The Blue Poems

The Blue Poems

DAVID C. CUSHMAN

Over Our Heads
Publishing

Copyright © 2023 by David C. Cushman

All rights reserved. Published in the United States by Over Our Heads Publishing. No part of this book may be reproduced in any form or by any electronic or mechanical means, including information storage and retrieval systems, without written permission from the author, except for the use of brief quotations in a book review.

ISBN: 978-0-9855674-8-4

*To those who are bold enough to pick up this book
and inspired to open it
and realize I was expecting them to...*

Ode to a Feeling	1
Rose	4
Born Through Tears	7
Memory Mothers	8
Soul Dog	9
Love's Pool	11
Credo	13
Brooding beauty	16
School Bus Vignette	17
Late Night	20
The Petition	23
Country	24
Jones's Memory	27
Norfolk Cliff	28
Duet for Hate	31
A Classic Composer	32
Muir Woods	36
Mine Memories	38
Daily Living Steadily Dying	39
44	41
Meditation	42
Mountain Memory I	45
Mountain Memory II	46
I Thought I Saw Her	47
Filing cabinets	48

Extend Your Hand	49
Steele but Ice Moving	52
Ponder a Moment	53
Draughty Winds	54
Grey Owl Eyed Woman	55
Left By Letting Go	58
Chain	59
Airport Wheelchair	60
From the Cave	63
Spirits Dwell	64
Tins of Time	65
Latent Leather	66
Summer Talk	67
Slowly Time	68
The Pushing Entry of One	72
I Dwell	73
Winter's White	74
Old Master Paints	76
MJ's Love, Love Goodbye	77

Ode to a Feeling

Ode to a feeling that won't be expressed
Cluttersome words, bothersome phrases
pins to destroy beauty
staking a feeling out, making
it stark
Ideas like butterflies, silken, colorful
full of flight
Die in a word, fade beneath
chloroforming syntax
Canned in a glass vessel, fragile
and stinking
flutter briefly and sink against
the smothering cotton
So I stay immobile, I stay calm
My ideas die, smashed beneath punctuation
But in the jar a moment cries
short beautiful life
And I see it exist for a second, as beauty
even as it dies
My knowledge surmises
A lot of words, and perhaps a gram of
meaning
But on the meaning
capable of blunting the pin

DAVID C. CUSHMAN

Leading, hopefully to more

oh, my love, my love, I hunger

The Blue Poems

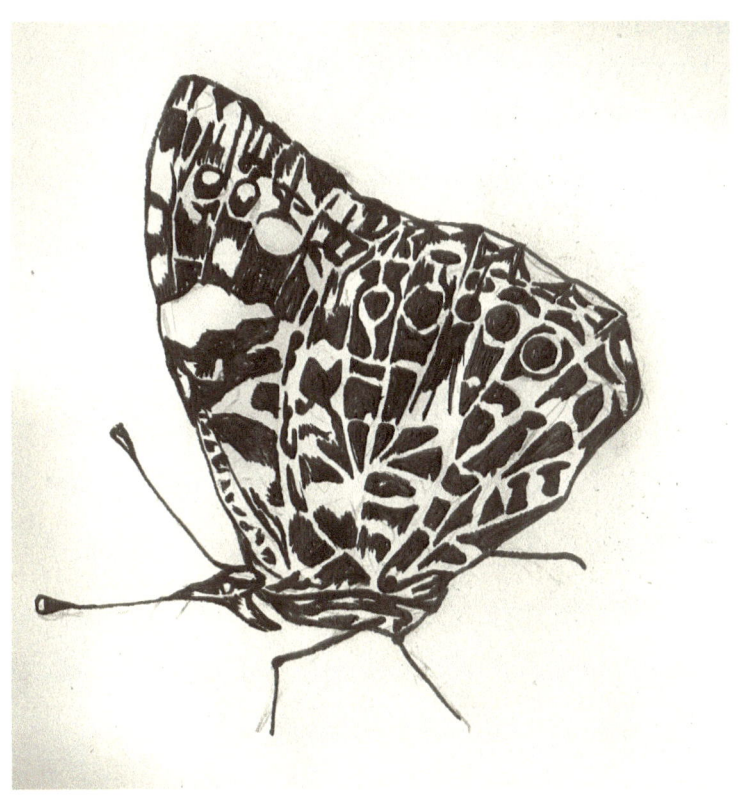

Rose

The smoothness of rock eroding
wind
Sky - in - depth
defies
sinking eyes that roved
in the procession of angular
faces.

She sought novelty
buying the wretched
passing all from hand to
                hand.

Took the stars to
shake,
    blasted a mind
or two
    starting a flesh quake.

Passing on with flexed
hips
and standard else where
a pennant she is
waving
from

The Blue Poems

a molding minaret

but oh

    oh

        her in sky depth

DAVID C. CUSHMAN

Born Through Tears

She arrived at the gate found a seat and began
to wait.
In time she made a call and when done
stiffened in her seat and began to weep.

A stranger brought her tissues and the others
around her turned their heads to hear the
explanation.
Her tears and sobs blocked her voice and she
could not produce a sound.

The call to board came and she rose her hand
against her chest as the sobs and tears ended.
She came by me to the boarding area. As she
passed, her lost eyes glanced at me and I saw
unshed tears still there.

I wondered had she seen me waiting and
crying earlier as I penned stanzas about a
woman in a wheel chair. Those tears had
birthed that poem.

Her tears birthed this one.

Memory Mothers

I have two memory mothers.

The first greets guests from the the stair landing back wall,
on their way to the second floor hall.

The second one adorns my mind.
Accessorizing me as my eternal companion hidden in the
iambic beat of my heart.
The one on the wall came from my daughter's early portrait
art.

The other, from life forever vows and the death
that ended my love's breath
in my ears and her fragrance that used to linger on my skin.

Now I breathe her into this poem and open memories with
gentle words to have her presence on this page. I'm a
minute hand

today I'm a minute hand
     trembling as smooth jewels pivot
     a marking time
     a timing mark
     that dimples
     round watch faces

Soul Dog

soul dog brown black
        eyes strong ears weak
        flop with careless paw
        on a colored veranda ears to twitch lazily to
        a fly fandango
        dust settles with fur
        and cursing fleas give you hell

DAVID C. CUSHMAN

Love's Pool

    Occasionally love's pool spouts with trout
    placid surface ripples with a life that explodes
        hooked
    barb embedded secure flopping on shore
    drowning in the air
    sometimes a trout comes to be in love's pool

a story of ripples, wavelets and curls

DAVID C. CUSHMAN

Credo

Your terms or mine
blind to perfection
accepting fault
blind for
a long
haul
-All-

                                        Leading chorales of
                                          strengthy singing
                                                      with
                                    shivers and simplicity.
                                  Voices creep with the
                                                    sand
                                    seeping to an ear

                  Reaching its
                    blindness.
                  A balm and balsum
                  psalm
                  rhythmic to a point
                  and then like a ringing

DAVID C. CUSHMAN

quoit
glancing from its stick
breaking to crescendo
-ah-
        miss
                      take this
for your own, knowing
that terms
your or mine are
only commending contracts.

The Blue Poems

Brooding beauty

Brooding beauty filling the slaked sky
rustled gentle susceptible trees
her passing sun-lit breeze
In the shaked air
A star began to tear
with its pin head light
a bright memory - hole.
Wish, Trish! Wish upon the tail
of the fish.
First to see
last to be
In shimmering, bursting sky
these stars would be the last to die

School Bus Vignette

Little girl probably eight rushing for the bus stop
just a tiny bit late.

Her haste due to time spent
getting ready, dressed, and eating quickly
to leave to go where she needs to go.

Expectant hulk of yellow bus stopped
Stairs and open door welcoming.

Then closing and the bus moving
and gathering its speed faster
than she seems to see
and still she rushes on
to where it will be.

Before she knows the bus goes
to where she needs to go
without her.

This morning no face appears
in the rear back window
to see the little one
with a late start

and a racing heart
just a bit broken now.

The Blue Poems

Late Night

Puddled pulsated desire
a hair hunger, a long
      moment sliding together
      in flesh knot
      of legs
            arms
      and
      lips
            that linger
and insect thoughts
            lacquered shiny green
glisten in blasting eyes
            while twining twosome
tear time and spear spans
      that cry
      passing,
      nothing ever passes
but coming love
      and past is
      split
            and shattered
      and seed is spread
            seeping towards matted
      sheet centers
            and cry

The Blue Poems

eyes
        that glistens
and pass
        to sleep, my long love

DAVID C. CUSHMAN

The Petition

We the undersigned, under siege
        and pummeled
        in fleshy runnels, protest
        this test of
        good man its
        as an end
yet,
        pet
                itch
                      ion
plea, berrenity happy Legatees of nucleic blight
we, undersigned
demand
Lett
        uce
        Be
        blind

Country

Drawlin' doggrel, barrel stomach Jones
his guitar
slashing
into spillin' drills
of rhythm,
spat as he squatted
in the shade.
rough walls, low halls of
a timbered barn
echoes his last
chorus
in the glinty eyes
of a barn rat

Jones meal sack shirt covering
his skin
raises a voice to
cob webbed
dust that passes
spiraling in light tatters
our of the sun pierced roof

Jones alone cowed with work
head hoaned red
by clean heat

crowned by
rich clay
his whiskers
Low thorns

DAVID C. CUSHMAN

Jones's Memory

hulking, battered, and
still,
a wool shirt his imaged
tartan,
creaseless pants his
cavalry twill,
bones fleshed by age and
cares,
a few hairs
hang from the
grazing hand.
His scapulate cheeks parched by
the
draughty suns of age,
lank plank sitter
scans a drainage ditch
musing of the rich,
grey hair swept by clawed fingers
restless as the heart and
as useless.

Norfolk Cliff

Alone, browed rock, sea spurned,
        Blotched with clotted gull droppings.
Still hard against the wind's eye that
        Views the slow mournful
Deterioration of its slab
        Pastured rim surrendering its sway
At the edge, down to sea smashed rock
        The old chips of dying earth
Nestled in ground sand waiting
        The scoring sweet gouge of surf.

The infinite economy of rock wind-sea schisms marking
        Foam surfaced depths with white
To break in eroding, piercing drops,
        Against time's extremism
While life boat bones tremble below
        Nature mocking man strove with
Cliff blocks to build a light capped
        Pustule in the sea, beneath the frowning brow
The fog comes and wreaths the
        Headland with damp grey chill,
The block tower glows its
        Promethean ember to sea
Helpless as the ships
        Roll and split far below

The Blue Poems

On sand crushed-from cliff rocks.

The sure sea stroke, decapitating loose
      Strand, shredding around still jagged
Chunks, braced by mass, surges in
      Smashing rhythm to end height and weight

Processing ceaseless tons and gallons
      Mud machinery turns to suck strength
And return beauty with measured eradication.

_____O_____

DAVID C. CUSHMAN

Duet for Hate

Long love lay, Leaden in its deadly silence,
Crippled in grace and split from a heart
       in red shivers of borne children.

A man, a stark nonity, greedsome
Culler of desparate fields blanked by
       sunlight.

A woman full of pressing loin needs
Riddled by lanky seeds and the octagonal
       loneliness.

Decides
in
a
seconds sounding to begin again.

A Classic Composer

What was it like to be a classic composer
And to know as the written sounds were letting
Go that beauty was all
To write in the clear light of dimming sight
Struggling to see with mind's ear
      the perfect notes

Here a clarion
                              Horns resound as
      there a viola

The pages appear
      in gentle procession harmonies
      found, arch and swirl from a
      pen
      ink filled piccolo, flutes and
      bassoons sing in the candle's
      light

Structuring scrawls of measures and bars, refining a
Symphony to the public taste with arrows joy.
Love glimmers as timpani skins shiver in morning eyes.

Words wielded as clubs echo in tuned kettles
      percussive thoughts rule the scale

Diminutive horns spout beneath the
drumming blows as swelling cat strings
sing
        of rhapsody
                of hope
Of loss
        of strength
                of loneliness

Could you composer, choose but one
And end your work

    Striking your harp
    Folding your papers
        and retiring with a parting
        glance at that scribbled pile
    to your silent bed.

Silent lump burnt out ember
        why sit in the dust of past fires
    no heat can stir
        those shiny facets to red burning
        stares in the banked hearth
Once superfluity, no dearth claims love's burning
Place
    scraps of charred paper
    consumed logs remnants of

past memories when full flames throttled season

But when all was consumed where could the fire
go but out.

The Blue Poems

Muir Woods

So close to the path you can touch and hold it without leaving the path. I believe they will populate my imagination and subconscious and remain recognizable until I end. They never do and appear to be as close to eternal life as we can perceive in our world.

The Blue Poems

Mine Memories

Mines splitting sandstone spines
of habited hills
Opened for a whim
to draw coal beds out.
Leering long hollows are
cat
      a
             combed with poisoned pine
uprights. Back pressing roofs
crush
      the helmet lights
            to pin points of
hazed gold. Mud and calming
drip of water embalm spirits
of
      fund
          a
             mental men and women
who live above.

Daily Living Steadily Dying

To give	To take	To receive
To live	To die	To conceive
To break	To glide	To guide
To make	To phrase	To quake
To provide	To praise	To forsake
To abide	To stride	To deride
To rise	To devise	To surprise
To reveal	To conceal	To seal
To deal	To hold	To mould
To create	To enfold	To desecrate
To shed	To gain	To attain
To share	To dare	To care
To claim	To blame	To bare
To name	To reclaim	To bear
To survive	To strive	To thrive

"Turn Turn" and "Both Sides Now"

Recovery
Discovery

The mountains burst from the sea
Rising to the clouds spontaneously
Displacing the sea surge over the old land sweeping

and drowning all living things.

The new sea over the old land fills with the charnel richness of nutrition for the new creation.

On the newly risen mountain slopes and peaks the sea waters run downward in ocean bound creeks and rivers.

Descending to the rocks and sands of the new table land.

Perishing sea species carried in the mourning salt tears down the new mountain sides and merge into the new tides of the new seas.

To lose	To gain
To seek	To hide
To bury	To exhume
To wish	
Endless	Eternal
Finite	Life
Death	Transformation

44

Saw 44, but only 10 lay now in their
        Black killing clothes.
        Thirty four nobodies M-16 bait
                Gone.
stumpy enemy barrels chatter,
        Fatal flute in a jungle symphony.
        Two go down, one silent
        the other in a delirium of sun
            Twists as butlers burrow
            Pain paths that hold him
        Centrally in a gradual vortex
        That fades to a twitch.
We got 22,
                Twelve nobodies.
They got 2
        Certain curtain curtailing
            2 sumbodies.

Meditation

The breath arrives then stays inside and then departs.
The fragrance remains along with the sound of the arriving breath.

A new fragrance remains with the departing breath.
A cleansing breath weaves into the new fragrance
as one heart and two lungs drive the flow from
> head
> to
> toe.

Peace slips gently into a thigh.
Joy enters an ear.
Serenity descends from an eyelid
and drains into a pupil.
Gratitude ascends through the floor into the stomach.
All functions in harmony and completely.

While the brain sleeps untethered,
thoughts and associations
arrive and depart without repetition
as Kharmaic surprises in the subconscious.

The mats and benches creak
as the sitters seek to move minutely

without distracting others.

The lotus fragrance pervades the air
as the peace blossoms
within each seeker.

Unified respiration pulls the air
without resistance into all.

Communal spirit glows purple
and detaches a new fragrance
for all to draw in
as the self flickers then goes out.

Mountain Memory I

Greying mountains standing in winter's age braced against
      the wind that drives the cloud fleece through the
trees
Littered by pine and constricted by concrete boas
Old hills rivened with wild erosive gullies and crumbling
rocks
      show lovely slow signs of dying.

      Men came with heavy punching tools to burrow a
short   cut
      And left the snake of white pavement coiled on the
            mountain's flank.
      Four lane bandages that bind the summit's wound
with a
            medial strip of stunted trees.
      The interstate plunges in directed greed through the
            mountain side.

Under winter's gasp of snow breath heavy tractor trailers
grind
      upgrade belching their pollution into the trees.

Mountain Memory II

In sovereign loneliness the grey hazed mountain lies twisted with
> the sclerosis of age in the snow light.

Above shriveled granite roots mica buds blossom as covering soil
> washes in centennial snow melt through a plunging gully.

In ancient pock pits pools sparkle sheened with ice reflecting
> weathered fire scarred trees.

In the spinning snow flake dance the coroner sky shrouds the
> moribund bulk with blank snow strewing clouds.

I Thought I Saw Her

For a moment of lovely drunk I thought I saw her
for a moment of deep boweled pain I did
and the blinding colors of rain slit sun
hid her skin, mottled by the spiking bed of
grass
water ran in flesh seated niagaras her tipped
precipices of breast
        trembled by the cool of passion and
        shrinking to a pimpled erectness of
        chilling strength
        paroxysms she coughed
        head bobbing in wearied droops that
        made me fold the blanket
dew soaked rain rolled and slithery with want
we hung together in prayerful arch and blasphemous
break
        prayerful arch   prayerful break
        /   \   /
blasphemous arch   blasphemous break
    seeing her below
        feeling her go
      slowly evasively coming
                as the rain sprinkled
into my shoulders steaming in the glen

Filing cabinets

Filing cabinets of mountains,
        cabins habited by cabinet filers
cabinet filers hinting at the folder forest
           lurking fillers slash at graceful doe fingers
               index carded foliage crinkles with the breeze
        of swift sealing
                    slam look under m
                 not there try u
flue caressingly over me
               bracing skies with tendrils of bacon smoke
contributing grey to the blue

Extend Your Hand

Extend your hand whenever you can to your fellow man
                    and include in your hand your soul, your life,
and your   faith.
Give your hand whenever you can to your fellow man
                    and include in your hand your past pain,
misery, and   confusion so he can
see those afflictions in himself.
Provide your hand anytime you can to your fellow man
       by reaching out to him through his pain, misery, and
                confusion and help him to enter the
solution.

Extend your hand whenever you can
       mustering your courage and spirit and giving all you
can
       and at times all you have.
Give your hand rejoicing that you can
       to your fellow man who trembles and sweats,
       and swears at you.
Turning sad demon eyes on you, he stares as you grip his
hand.

Provide your hand anytime you can
       and know its your measure as a recovering man.
Extend your hand to a down on his luck fellow man.

A higher power takes away your fear and expectation.

As you extend your hand inspirations flow into your fellow man   and settle into the shadows of his pain and despair.
There they stay in your fellow man
     awaiting the day to blossom from the program's cultivated   ground bringing love to his heart and light to his spirit.
Then sweetly later, the words close to a needed song spring from his mouth as he extends his hand to his fellow man
     who needs a hand from a fellow man.

The Blue Poems

Steele but Ice Moving

Steele but ice moving /on sundered stillness
white roller river /pocked with gathered stone
spired by pressure needles /its way to mountain feet
sipping two feet of sod /freezing decay coldly crumbling
the glacier begins its melting slide /pushing in its frigid
                            tide
                          the pine hill aside

Ponder a Moment

Ponder a moment said the hour
houri time sinuous
      rhythmic, a belly dance
from the stance of the triple cock
crew cut denials riding with the
cross
      striding helmets plumed for blood
loomed on the white weave of agony
galloping navel a swiftly curtained cyclops
silver shivering in the sun falls to the
stage
thrown
while the parade paused
halted by fleshy gyres
thorn and splinter brushing each other
a debate
both agree
and enter the spilling skin
one soldier
wants another look
com' on she's thin
and the moment starts again

Draughty Winds

Draughty winds of passing years can not
        change the charcoal slashes of twin shadows
        fading in the dusk
                Even now there comes another
                and another and yet another,
                until all are gathered forming
                the shadow wheel of a family
                reveling in the sun

Grey Owl Eyed Woman

grey owl eyed woman
A Goddess for forest love
A tawny dove, a precipiate
emotion
Love —
flee head long, heels flashing
invitations to a hunt
Hunting for a soul, a soul-mate's
love.
Strings beckon and jerk
beneath the hands
We chase and snap, and
love again.
Again a run, a thrashing
and rabbits dart
And beneath the slice'ed bole
we part

A surcease, that can not
be stood
A pause that drives us from
peace
Oh, Diana; a bliss, a
nerveless pain, I cry
names chords and tears

Beset upon in your native
brush
Your bow-string frayed and
useless
Fleetly lithe thighs carried
you away

The Blue Poems

Left By Letting Go

Her fingers on my wrist moved and gripped,
her last touch as her only breath left ended.

A minute and then 2 passed,
When I looked at her face,
She had slipped away peacefully to her next place
On Eternity's chain.
Truly missed now, of her presence only ashes, photos, and memories remain.

Beneath the shading trees over our patio,
At the end of our last run together,
we sat side by side 11 years ago
and let our hearts slow.

Conversing in voices soft and low,
We spoke of joy, children, grandchildren,
Stopping work, and laughed at the last.
Truly blessed

Chain

When my wife leaned back and raised her eyes to the sky, she could see beyond the atmosphere to the skies beyond ours.

Her imagination fired by the writings of C.S. Lewis, Jules Verne, Ray Carpenter, and other writers of science fiction would command her eyes to go beyond our universe to the endless chain of universes.

We would talk once she went through to those other skies, each one more distant with no walls or limits.

Her smile incandescent as she told her thoughts and beliefs to me about the infinite and our souls eternally linked.

Cloud burst passes for the day with my careful cache of feelings, like all things hidden surfacing unbidden and then ascending from solitude in a prayer of gratitude for all given, granted, and provided.

Airport Wheelchair

Hopeless, helpless, less than ever before, a woman confined to an airport wheelchair propelled by a stranger follows behind a purposeful crowd moving rapidly towards the boarding gate.

The wheelchair and its passenger propelled by the stranger rolls across the floor towards the spot

where the chair passenger and the passenger's husband will wait for their special boarding call.

He is a step or two away from being by her side

She glances to the right and glimpses his confident stride that she once matched.

The chair slows, the stranger hasn't spoken and the chair bound wife wonders as her anger seethes if the stranger pities her.

It's the chair, the stranger has propelled so many while doing her job.

Always in this chair, the same chair with different
passengers always working behind their backs to get them
there as quickly as she
can.

She now feels the weight of the woman in the chair as she
pushes the chair and its cargo to the spot.

The husband bends slightly to speak to his wife
and then turns and strides confidently towards a distant
news stand
unable to sense that his wife has started a conversation with
Death.

DAVID C. CUSHMAN

From the Cave

From the cave, I write again of red woods
and giants beyond our understanding,
but within our scope of acceptance.
A willingness surges through our minds
carrying all before to a barred door
and when enough pressure arrives
splitting its aged wood apart
for us to enter.
In the broad hall,
the walls rise on either side and curl in to an arched roof
baffling the sea salt winds that strive to regain strength
and breach the red wood grove
where her soul resides.
Solitude grows daily as do the trees in the grove.
Azure moods flow around eddies of love
near the path into the grove.
And the unknowable energy grows.

Spirits Dwell

I am telling the world the spirits dwell here
and humans get well here
from sadness
and cross paths with memories
from this grove that existed
hundreds of years before
we left the wombs that bore us
and now our predecessors still remain straight and strong
greeting us daily
questioning what's wrong
and removing our dark woe with dancing light
so bright
it pierces our rods and cones
and leaves us blinded with sight.

Tins of Time

Tins of time, sardined rows
      coffins laid angularly
to the prevailing wind
      baring the bone smell
of rest. Eroding flesh pulse by dinning
      time rippled ebbing to the hard
scapulate flats of calcium
      listing white shards stick and gouge the
stinking velvet
      terminal rhythm roundhousing the
tedial souls that these brass
      shellswill cost in metal
weight and wood handled luxury.

Latent Leather

Latent leather grained by machine,
crackles and settles beneath the warm weights
soft sucking sounds—
kisses
But then the cold vinyl is slippery
and her back slides down
slumps
arms rise and fall in mute delight
legs twine to hold hardened waist
Brief motions turn minds to another
Reeling worlds center in her eyes
Shut
Gentle insinuation, perfect sensual
relaxation.
The back creaks and couch legs shiver.

Summer Talk

Summer talk in low slow circles of haze slips among the trees. Green bound lovers roll pressing their heat into the flattening grass. We climb a crackling hill. Mounting against the bright pines with winking branches the lake opens below. Chill blueness rises in wide breaths cooling our skin and mingling with silence
      fly punctured hums, pests rip our peace
          Plunging in our fall towards
                shimmering concrete
                      and blighted air
    Return, wish we could, to
    flattened weeds. Behind us, those supine
    angel moulds melt in the
    headland wind

Slowly Time

Slowly time ran bubbling through my hand
I made a fist and it squirted hissingly into the sand
I stared
watching my love cross to the bar
white arms wink in the grey swell
and the ocean smoke delivers its smell
Now she stands
straight in a latex's bond
whitely waving
      above the water's surge

Time moves her feet
      in morassed shell and weed
I stay ashore
she beckons, she cries
squinting against the sun
she swats a horse fly.
I stay ashore
feet in dry sand
grasping joyfully at time
flowing from my hand

When she comes to land
should I fling this flowing
endless stuff to the air

to glitter there.

Gone in a leap to her side
grasp her wet to my chest
ignore the taste of salt grit
and prey upon her soft lip

Yet I stay ashore alone
watching the ocean rine foam on the beach
fish carcass drift and bump with the
pulsing wave,
the hand built nave of a sand cathedral.
Black vegetable blobs squash obstructively in my hand
while the garbage floats in.

And time coarse of grain is blocked
my fingers squeeze into prayer lock
staying on the crowded shore.
Blistered bodies lumping under domed
canvas for shade
guards squint over the grey face
whistles sound
rollers groan
       the boat is rushed to the sea

Out beyond the seventh crest a head bobs
and starts to swim

now two bob and two gesture desparately
the boat thrashes near
finally the bronze young man leaps
but the white cap is gone.
And I stay ashore alone

The Blue Poems

The Pushing Entry of One

The pushing entry of one
        time slow pulsing
        soul into another
        with the disparate
        unity
                emerging of self
        against self
Elfine shoes of
        worlds brimming
        with life
        blossomed from anger
        enriched with
        half hidden tears
        and buried within
                sad rock by
The mushroom sheltered
        circle of dry grass widows
        squaring their rotundity
        for their daily pretense
        at gaity
        all thoughts rising
        from that solitary
        past quarrel starring
                ourselves.

I Dwell

I dwell in these woods within dreams I can not recall
and now I find serenity in a wall
and that's not all,
you see what you wanna see in the woods
and it stamps the words
eternal love
with reality.

Winter's White

Winter's white prairie rolls
    in swells of chill
        air
            capping pines and
                mountains.
Hills crackle in crisp
    moon pale as
        ice grows from
           thawing eaves
                and the freeze
                    begins

Mounded lumps
    with antenna spiking
        litter parking lots
            and blue exhaust
                floats to the ground
    scoured raw in the wind
hands wrap shovels handles
    in lifting and thrusting
        the greying snow away

Dancing voices of children
    blend with the hiss of plastic bag slides
        on and down the

The Blue Poems

                gleaming hillsides
Wrapped in clotted ice after rolls
      to dodge posts and trees
           the children gather
                     warming themselves with laughter

Old Master Paints

Artist skies sketched by jets as night begins with pink tinted cloud edges and our home skies become a feat of our old Master's brush as He presses the strokes upward toward the top of the alabaster dome.

He labors long to get it right to catch the arriving night in the fading light.

He takes indigo and octopi ink and mixes in fragrance of rose.

While below charnel vaults sealed and full with the dead echo with the scrape of shovels and rattle of brittle bones.

I think the old Master someday will decide enough painting has occurred to meet the needs of eternity.

MJ's Love, Love Goodbye

Faith leads to the Heart of everything
       and that is the creator of only one thing
       and we call that eternity.
In the Heart of everything we find eternity.
In our own heart we discover faith
       in simple ways as we travel each day's journey
       along eternity's chain.

When she passed we took hold of her with grief
We claimed her again for our selves after letting go.

We tried to bind her with our sadness to memorialize
       her dazzling smiles in our memory files.
We tried to speak by telephone into her solitude
       and told her our wonderful things
       and dreams
       and bargained with her to stay
       by telling her she could go.

Now her time has passed a full year
       and like lichen on a rock
       or the rock itself
       we cling to the memories that remain here.
Our sorrowful thoughts like hot brands

    inscribing our hearts with longing left us bereaved.

Yet she had let go of us altogether
    as her heart stilled and her breath whispered
    away that day
    she soared to eternity.
She shows the way as our eternal teacher to give everything
    and accept eternity in its place.

I can accept that today
    and twirl and whirl some days hence
    in dances of joy,
      and in this tear sodden shirt feel her peace flow
        in to the loving heart inside mine.

My deepest thanks to my family, my friends, and especially to Kelly for listening to my poetic wanderings through the years.

Book cover designed by Isobel Dowdee
Butterfly drawing by Fiona Dowdee
Photography by Gwyneth Dowdee
Frog drawing by Ean Dowdee

These poems were compiled and formatted and published by the poet's daughter — the author Diana Knightley.

(Thank you, Dad, for the honor of reading them.)

The Frog goes into the bar and says, "Bartender give me a whisky sour!"

The Bartender says, "Here you go, frog," and places the drink in front of the frog.

The Frog picks it up and drinks it completely in one gulp,

and then
    falls off
        the barstool
            and then
                croaks.

—DCC

www.ingramcontent.com/pod-product-compliance
Lightning Source LLC
Chambersburg PA
CBHW032047290426
44110CB00012B/986